Touching the Serpent's Tail

by

MICHAEL ROBINSON

Martin House Publishing, R.R.#1, Keene, Ontario K0L 2G0   (705) 295-4491

Designed and printed by Commercial Press, Peterborough, Ontario

Canadian Cataloguing in Publication Data

Robinson, Michael, 1948 -
  Touching the Serpent's Tail

ISBN No. 0-9695225-1-7

1. Indians of North America - Poetry. I. Title.
PS8585.0356T68 1992   C811'.54   C92-094181-8
PR9199.3.R628T68 1992

Martin House Publishing, R.R.#1, Keene, Ontario K0L 2G0   (705) 295-4491

Dedicated to my children,

Rebecca

Zachary

Joshua

Alecia

Illustrations

Contents

Touching the Serpent's Tail

I was living in the Eagles time,
watching, high from the back
of the sleeping snake.
Below me, the water moves in rhythm,
rising and falling
to the Serpents sweet song,
pushing me onward,
like a leaf in the wind...
holding me to the Eagles wings,
as he flies on,
chasing the sun.

The contrast between
the silver white of the water
and the black rocks and trees,
blind the birds' eyes,
erasing the reality
of shoreline and sea,
redefining it as 'day
and night'.
He flies as a dream-maker.
A weaver of chance.

As I watch,
his shadow suddenly breaks away
becoming its own master,
with no path of its own
to follow.
It silently slips away into the black,
to quench its thirst
for its own identity.
High above, the Eagle flies on
in a thunderstorm of agony and tears;
like a mother looking for its lost child.

A night fire beats
deep inside of me
as I race madly
through the black night,
following the shadow-bird
on his quest to nowhere.

In another time,
another place,
I sit quietly in my canoe
and listen.
I can hear their strange voices
in ancient tongues
echoing though the ravens call.

They move in their long canoes
like ghosts
across the bay.

Their rhythmic paddling
sounds like bird wings
beating against the water,
trying to break its hold
to fly free.

I sit alone
by my fire,
surrounded by these lonely men,
who like me,
passed this spot
on the back of the Serpents tail.

They talk long into the night,
with bits of fire and mold
falling from their mouths.
They seem to be waiting.
Suddenly,
they point to me
with accusing fingers,
demanding me to identify
myself,
to explain why I am here,
sitting at their fire!
When I at last
find my voice to speak,
they have gone.
All I hear
is the distant surf,
and the pounding of my own heart.

Out in the black night
the Serpent sleeps.
Above me,
giant wings cross the heavens.
For a brief movement
its shadow crosses my eyes
and I am a bird...
I am a shadow,
seeking to find my soul.

The water lay still
in a chorus of smoldering fire.
The land around was heavy and dark.
The towering trees
stood ghost-like,
silent statues,
blocking out the night sky.
They were the ancient children,
watching for strangers
to pass.
Waiting for souls to drift by,
to enchant them to stay,
trapping them for eternity.

The shadows were alive.
The black trees and rocks
were mirror images
of a time gone by.
They seem so still,
untouchable...
as they watch the ghostly shadows

above the still water,
climbing and falling,
murmuring,
moving back and forth,
in a strange slow dance.
This was their time,
their place
and I am the stranger
passing
on a silver line,
leaving only tiny whirlpools
of bubbles
behind me,
that quickly erase any evidence
of my being there.
Above my head
flutter a thousand tiny moths,
ghosts of long ago travelers,
whispering,
calling out,
'Who are you?'
Each paddle stroke
echoes like a soft
flutter of wings,
in time with my own
beating heart,
giving the illusion
of being followed.
Somewhere ahead I see
a fire,
small and bright.

A tiny window
on the black wall
of this strange night.

I slowly stop
and look back.
There was nothing
but black night
and the strange sense
that I have passed
this way before.

I knew then
that I had touched
the Serpent's tail.

The Rabbit Man
and the Ghost

When I look,
I see only movement
and shadows.
When I sing,
I hear only thunder
and the beating
of a moth's wings.

A Time When the River Was Real

A Time When
the River Was Real

There was a time when the sky was still,
but no one was aware that everything had
changed.
No one could hear the river.

High on the cliffs,
the priests sang all night.
Singing into the future,
like ancient mad men,
yelling into a mirror.
They knew why no one could hear the river.

When one of the spirit men left the cliffs,
he met a bear.
The bear greeted him kindly.
"I did not know a bear could speak my
language," the priest answered.
"I did not know a man could speak mine," said
the bear.

In Her Grandfather's Mountains

In Her Grandfather's Mountains

The mountains do not promise security or
beauty.
They do not claim to be right or wrong;
to be a master or slave.
They live beyond the reach of logic or reason.
They are tiny slivers of light,
the edges of clarity.
They are huge islands of power.
'Caves', where the spirit of life, can hide its true
identity,
so it may continue its journey into infinity.

The mountains are a battleground for warriors.
A desert to men with gray hearts.
A cold grave to men with no hearts.
But to her grandfather,
the mountains were a window to heaven.

Infinity and Clarity

Infinity and Clarity

T he earth is a mirror image of herself.
   Her energy, her life force, is like a river of silver
moths
rolling and fluttering across a history
of sunrises and sunsets.
Across an endless landscape of campfires and
dreams
of wandering hunters.
Her clarity, sparkling and dancing like ancient
dancers
at the edge of life,
race ahead of her history.
Leaving behind the smoke, the shadows of day and
night.
Good and evil.
Life and death and mystery.

The priests sang all night.
Singing into the fire.
They were fish, birds and bears.
And it was good.

The History and the Earth

The History and the Earth

T he Earth exists in the strength of the beads
  History placed around her neck.
Each bead is a moment in History.

But History imposed and built enormous
kingdoms and gods,
balanced on each bead,
like stepping stones across the universe.

Yet History failed to see the Earth's strength
was in the string
that held the endless silver beads
as one.
But when History's right side
imposed values
of such majestic height
that its eyes glazed over
with glory and dazzle...
the load become too great.
The string broke,
scattering the beads
across a black eternity.

The Old Man and the Hunters

The Old Man
and the Hunters

I am an ancient child,
alone, drifting in a cold lake
by the shores of mirrored rocks and doorways
made of smoke.
I am a moment of history,
a gray river that has no origins.
I am a hermit, a small butterfly in a shell of stone,
fluttering across an invisible land.

I hear the beaver cry.
He tells me his heart is on fire.
I hear the fish in the night.
He moves as a silent thought, a stranger in flight.
Above my head, the hunters soar,
the strong and the weak, side by side,
never stopping until one dies.
From sunrise to sunset,
life rolls like a ball of light, across the lake.
It is a lifetime in itself.
An entire history.
To some, it is just the beginning.
For others, there is no end.

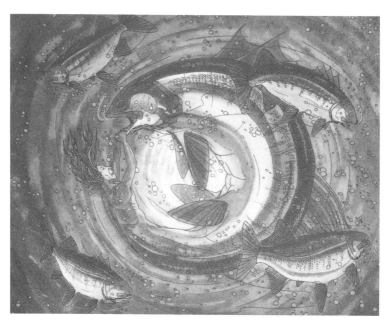

Changing Directions at the End of Seasons

Changing Directions
at the End of Seasons

His song was not mine,
yet He was one of us.
He became a stranger.
His eyes seemed alive,
but he had no heart.
When he spoke, his words fell
from his head like stones.
His words were sad and angry.
He was never a child.
At his death, he sang someone else's song.
He died an old man.
Outside his window
the spirits watched him leave,
then they swam away.

Life on the Moon

Life on the Moon

A man, trapped in life
sold all he owned
for a brief moment...
a once in a lifetime chance
to see his future...
To dance with it;
and live to tell about it.
It was a dangerous idea,
with enormous responsibilities
but he was not allowed pity
or compassion
as a partner
to peek into his future.

I watched the man, trapped in life;
a fool in a glass jar,
his face pressed up against the side,
like a child's face
against a toy store window.
Totally unaware of his existence,
unaware of his shaking hands,
of the cold glass.

Soon the wind will come
and drive the man away.
Leaving his glass jar behind,
broken and empty.

I am the wind on the moon
and must stay here.
Waiting for the spring,
waiting forever.

The Nowhere Song

The Path of Life
is a road to nowhere.
It is a balance
between insanity and reason.
It waits for no one.
Promises nothing.
Yet nothing else exists,
except the Path.

Listening to the Night

Listening to the Night

L ook for the bird
that isn't a bird,
but walks with the legs
of a man.
Listen for the stranger
who taps the stones
by the creek,
with the dream sticks
made of glass.
Look for the bird
with eyes of pearls,
that watch the ghosts
that live in the creek.

Don't point your finger,
like a bone stick,
at the Priest
singing in the dark.
Listen to the songs
that live in the shadows.
Listen to the silence,
as it flies
in huge circles
above the night.

The Sacred Fire

The Sacred Fire

In ancient times,
night was a crushing
separate reality.
It was a hovering black bird
from another world,
that divided
and drove away
any strength,
any decision
made in the day.

No fire was ever built
in the same place twice.
The fire-keeper,
a very nervous man,
always watched the horizon
with one eye
and the fire
with the other.
He never spoke
but only muttered.
He never slept.

The others would watch him
as though he was a God.
A man of mystery.
Soon they lost their ability
to watch the horizon.

The fire-keeper
once had a dream.
In his dream he saw a huge stone.
It was flying.
It was on fire.

Seed of Life

The hunter planted
a small bush,
hoping his gesture
would bring him good fortune.
But he was too busy
trying to draw attention
to his kind act,
that he forgot to water
the plant
and it died.

The Shadow of a Man

The Shadow of a Man

Once a week, for several months
he came to this place.
Here he talked and learned about
the 'shadow' of a man.
Each day he returned
as a different person,
for a different reason.
What he learned each day
was a gain, a step forward,
but to gain something
is to lose something,
and what was lost was never
discussed.
The man had now completely lost
his original identity.
He even lost his desire to talk.

It was a bit unnerving
when he realized
that for the last two visits
no words were spoken.
Now, as before,
he sat quietly, waiting
for the priest to begin.
Waiting for the day to end.
Watching his shadow grow longer.

The Song of the Hunter

The Song of the Hunter

'Beware,' sings the sparrow.
'You are growing smaller
and smell like the wind.
Your shadow
lies behind you, alone,
exposed on the desert floor,
open to the hunters
in the sky.'
'Beware,' sings the sparrow.
'You are turning
into smoke and rust.
You sat and watched
as the King burst
into flames.
You watched as the flames
spread into the bush,
exploding into a huge ball of fire.
But you leapt to your feet,
screaming,
When the fire devoured
your homes.
Then you spent the night
blaming the King
for your loss.'

'Beware,' sings the sparrow
from his small cage.
'I have little water
or food left.
Soon I will have
to look to the King
for help.'

Justice of an Idea

It is cold and very dark.
You feel cheated.
Yet you are the one
who turned out the light.

Survival of the Hunter

Survival of the Hunter

The hunter was invisible,
hiding in the safety of distance,
far from the war cry
and enemy faces.
Living in the shadow
of a fire,
that was far too big
for a summer day.
Too hot to be so close.

The hunter was scared
as he hid behind his weapons.
Searching for words
to allow him
to escape the reality
of becoming what he hunted.
To leave the security of the fire.

Watching the Hunters

Watching the Hunters

They watch from the trees.
They can be anything
they want,
but destiny
made them birds..,
watchers with silver eyes.
Strange little men,
who use the trees
as doorways
to other worlds.

I watch them
and they watch me.

The Earth

The Earth

I drift alone
in my black night...
in my silence.
I am light years
apart
from my sisters.
I am alone,
in pain,
unable to give birth.
My heart aches
as my soul
and my shadow
cling to my breast
like frightened children.

I long to hear
the eagle,
to watch him fly.
To lie in spring grass
and listen to the wind.
I long to leave,
to be a part
of the black silence.

The Singer

The Singer

The Singer stood
in the river.
It was on fire.
The river flowed
around the earth
like a silver ribbon.
Its path was decided
long ago.

His words are
old,
like tiny birds
that hover above the river.
His words
are silent,
like shadows
made of water
that are invisible
in the river.

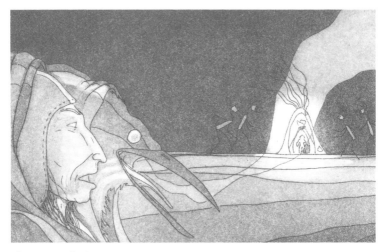

The Priest and History

The Priest and History

To be invisible, is to have
no secrets to blind you,
to confuse you.
To be invisible, is to be lost
from the world
of order and fear.

To be invisible, is to be
in two places
at the same time.
And only you know
where the two places are.

To be invisible, is to be
a wisp of smoke at night.
A song of secret words.
An ordinary man with no history.
A child who smiles with his eyes,
whose heart is the wind.

To be an invisible fire,
is to be free
to roam the universe
as a tiny moth.
Free from the nets
of the blind men.

There is only one duty left,
for a man whose shadow is pure light.
He must cloak himself
in silence
and rush into the sky,
looking for eternity.

Leaving the Sky

"I heard the trumpet sing,"
cried the eagle,
"and as it came closer,
I realized it was not a bird.
It left a gray shadow
across the sky,
blocking out the sun.
It made me wish
I was not a bird."

A Drifting Moment of Grace

A Drifting Moment of Grace

The blind hunter sat in the dark,
listening to the old man talking.
"Your problem is your fear
of making choices," the old man said.
"Choices you can't see.
But choice is a reality, it is your life.
You for you,
hiding away in your nighttime.
It is bound by a balance of your perceptions
or the lack of them,
and by your own history."
"But I am blind!" pleaded the hunter.
"To be blind, is not your mistake.
It is your spirit that is gone.
It has left through your eyes
and has left black holes
in your head.
While your spirit remains lost,
the holes are left empty,
to be filled with wind and rain
and fear.
You have become
half a man.
You have become invisible."

The blind man was warned
again
about the water.
He only laughed
at the old speaker.
He laughed until he cried,
until his voice and fears
disappeared beneath the surface.
Soon it was though
he was never there.

The old turtle,
his face empty of expression,
slowly turned
and swam away.

Not far away
another hunter sat singing
to the night sky.
His eyes, like his name, were blurred,
and were slowly sinking.
He could see no one
and no one could see him.

Knock on the Door

I sat beside a small creek,
watching the water moving past
on its private journey.
Bubbling, rolling, it moved by me,
as though I was not there.
My eyes drifted beneath
the surface.
I could see hundreds
of smooth pebbles.
Suddenly, as I watched,
the pebbles slowly changed
into faces.
Yelling out to me,
but the moving water
muffled their voices.

Keeper of a Dream

Keeper of a Dream

'The Keeper' is an ancient dreamer,
in an ancient tongue;
in an ancient time.
He is a smokeless fire
flickering in the black of night.
Hidden away
in a silent forest.

He moves slowly, in his dream,
across a pearl white sea.
A landscape of old men.
A place too old to carry pain
or regret.
Their blind eyes stare,
unblinking,
in the face of an angry sun.

The evening wind
is cool and relentless,
stalking the dying hearts
that wander away from the dream.
To steal them back,
to hide them among the rocks
and garbage.

The ancient dreamer
hovers like a hungry hawk
above the sleeping dream
waiting for its spirit
to wake
to light the pipe
and smoke.

The Price of Kindness

I touched the blindman's arm
and asked if I could help.
He jumped back
as though my hand
burned his arm.
In a loud voice,
he told me
that even though he was blind,
he could see more than me.
He lifted his head
and sniffed the air.
"You smell," he added,
"besides, I do not want to go anywhere."
He lay down and went to sleep.

Dancing Forever

Dancing Forever

For centuries,
there will be no history,
only small campfires,
only fear.

Don't point your finger
at the man
who thinks he is a tree.
He is the only one who is free.

Your dreams are bought
and stagnant,
locked away in your golden chest.

Your song is a dance
with no music,
no children
and no key.

Don't point your finger
at the Priest
you paid to bless your gold.
He is drunk,
turning to religion
to ease his pain.

His falling tears
burn holes in his heart.
The hunter is left
to fend for himself
as he crosses
the ibis of ignorance,
as the rich and powerful
take shots
at him,
as an afternoon sport.

For centuries
you will have to live
with your gold.

Dreams of Stone

I gave you a part of me,
but you took all of me,
as if it was your right.
I now lie cut open,
frightened,
exposed to
the wind and snow.
My heart is divided
from my spirit by a
wire fence,
My womb lies
buried,
full of stones...
My tears are silent,
frozen;
like bits of ice
clinging to the stars.
My future lies hidden
in my shadow.

My dreams are thunder.

Winter Fire

Winter Fire

I watched the shadows
of winter
drift in and around me,
like tiny bits of gray mist.

With the skill of thieves,
they slipped silently
between the fire
and my blankets,
between my fingers,
between my words.
They entered my head
through my eyes,
listened for a moment...
Then they were gone.

Metal Spiders

The three merchants of profit,
the gray entities from the house of pity,
from the city of masters and misery.

This elite group of blind men
stumble along in the dark,
selling the vision of light.
The promise of peace...
and are hailed and celebrated
by fools at every turn,
as Kings of civilized ideals.
For a small fee
you can stand in their shadows,
as a legacy
to be told and retold
to your grandchildren.

These gray men move quickly
from place to place,
to avoid any confusion with truth.
Rolling in the heart of a huge
dust storm.
A swirling dance, out of control.

These three Gods of fear
are the angels
of ignorance,
of apathy,
and greed.
They are driving the children
of the stars
into the oil river,
long before they can understand
their ability to choose.
Long before they can swim.

The three merchants push on
relentlessly,
changing the rules of life and death
at every whim,
at every chance
and game of profit.

The mothers of all creatures
of life
are left behind, alone
abused
and forgotten.
Their spirits torn open
and cold.
Their bodies left empty
to the birds of the night
and the never ending dust.

The three self-appointed angels
continue their rolling journey,
crushing the life from the very rocks
beneath their metal boots.
Exposing the Earth's soft belly
to be scrapped away,
to be divided again and again.
To be made the prisoner.
A sacred moth,
with its wings torn away.

Within this new Kingdom,
there is no sunset,
no singing.
The eerie cry of a blackbird
is heard
echoing through the dust,
that never seems to settle.
The clarity of justice
is invisible.
Lost behind the grin
of the three Merchants of Profit

The Written Word

The Snake was on fire,
     as he lied
about who taught him
to dream.
The smoke blotted out the sun
as his words
tumbled from his mouth,
like tiny balls of fire
promising me
immortality
if I would stay
and listen to his story.
If I would let him
peek into my dreams.
Just for a moment.

Through the smoke,
I could see his grin
and his twitching
leather tongue.

Through the smoke
I could see his scaly hands
caressing the pearls
around his neck.

"Give me your hand" he whispered
and I'll give you a gift
that you can't refuse.

Canadian Best Seller

THE EARTH AND THE DANCING MAN

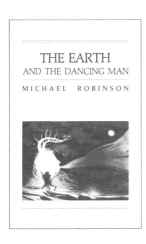

The earth never offered man
Water
As a gift

Water was part of her
It is her blood
Her moving force

And in this, she said
You will see your greed
Your mistakes
Your image
But few will see me.

(Reflections 1989)

THE EARTH AND THE DANCING MAN by Michael Robinson is available at your local bookstore or can be ordered direct from the publisher.

The Earth and the Dancing Man $14.95
Touching the Serpent's Tail $14.95

ADD $3.00 postage and handling. Send cheque or money order.

Name ....

Address ....

City .... Postal Code.........................

Martin House Publishing, R.R.#1, Keene, Ontario K0L 2G0   (705) 295-4491